The Double Bass, How It Works

The Double Bass, How It Works

A Practical Guide to Double Bass Ownership

Michael J. Pagliaro

Co-Published in Partnership with the
National Association for Music Education

ROWMAN & LITTLEFIELD
Lanham • Boulder • New York • London

Published by Rowman & Littlefield
An imprint of The Rowman & Littlefield Publishing Group, Inc.
4501 Forbes Boulevard, Suite 200, Lanham, Maryland 20706
www.rowman.com

86-90 Paul Street, London EC2A 4NE, United Kingdom

British Library Cataloguing in Publication Information Available

Library of Congress Cataloging-in-Publication Data

Names: Pagliaro, Michael J., author. | National Association for Music Education.
Title: The double bass, how it works : a practical guide to double bass ownership /
  Michael J. Pagliaro.
Description: Lanham : Rowman & Littlefield, 2023. | "Co-Published in
  Partnership with the National Association for Music Education." | Summary:
  "This book is designed to expand a student's music study experience by
  learning about the parts of the double bass and how it works, how to care for
  it, how it is made, its history, useful accessories, and how to plan practice
  sessions"—Provided by publisher.
Identifiers: LCCN 2022060311 (print) | LCCN 2022060312 (ebook) | ISBN
  9781475869163 (paperback) | ISBN 9781475869170 (epub)
Subjects: LCSH: Double bass—Maintenance and repair. | Double bass—
  Construction.
Classification: LCC ML920 .P34 2023 (print) | LCC ML920 (ebook) | DDC
  787.5/1928—dc23/eng/20221215
LC record available at https://lccn.loc.gov/2022060311
LC ebook record available at https://lccn.loc.gov/2022060312

♾™ The paper used in this publication meets the minimum requirements of
American National Standard for Information Sciences—Permanence of Paper
for Printed Library Materials, ANSI/NISO Z39.48-1992.

Table of Contents

Acknowledgments.. vi

Introduction... vii

Scientific Pitch Notation... viii

1. What Are the Parts of My Double Bass, and How Do They Work?.................. 1

2. How Do I Care for My Double Bass Outfit? 25

3. How Should I Plan My Practice Sessions? 35

4. What Items (Accessories) Will I Need to Help Me Play My Double Bass?.... 39

5. How Are Double Basses Made?.. 53

6. What Is the History of the Double Bass? 69

7. How Are Double Bass Bows Made?... 83

8. What Is the History of Bows? 89

9. A Dictionary for Double Bass Students 95

10. A Review of Double Bass Parts and Their Use 99

Index 107

Acknowledgments

The following extraordinarily gifted professionals in the field of musical instrument fabrication and distribution have generously granted permission to use information and artwork from their websites. Listed in alphabetical order, they are:

Donna Altieri Bags, info@altieribags.com.

bwlibys.blogspot.com, for the picture of a bow hair under a microscope.

PlayMusic123 (www.playmusic123.com) for content from their website.

Dr. Robin Deverich, for allowing the use of The Advanced Fingering Chart 1st - 7th Positions www.stringbassonline.com.

Steve Erling, Oceanside, CA, Thank you for your counsel and photos for How Double Basses are Made. www.highlandwoodworking.com.

Gollihur Music, Visit their extraordinary website at https://gollihur-music.com for the labeled diagram of the double bass in chapter 1.

Scott Hershey, master luthier at http://www.hersheyviolins.net

Eitan Hoffer, archetier extraordinaire, a specialist in the fabrication of ancient bows at http://www.hoffer-bows.com.

Christopher E. Kalish, Computer Scientist, for his help in dealing with the intricacies and mysteries of the computer world.

Lars Kirmser, publisher and musical instrument specialist at http://www.musictrader.com.

Heinrich Krutz, a contemporary luthier, for permission to use pictures from his website. info@krutzstrings.com.

Hubert de Launay, info@hubertdelaunay.com

Christine Patrice Raciti, consultant to the non-fretted string instrument industry. Thank you for your guidance on the details of double bass ownership.

Jenna M. Socci, —B.S. (Psychology), MPS (General Education and Special Education), for your guidance in establishing a suitable syntax to better communicate with younger students.

Otis A. Tomas, master luthier at www.otis@fiddletree.com.

Jimmy Sang Wang, bow manufacturer at http://www.wangbow.com.

Introduction

The method book you are already using was written to help you learn how to play the double bass. That book contains information on holding your double bass, making a sound, reading music, playing different notes, and much more.

This companion book will teach you additional information about your instrument that will help you better understand how it works, how to work it, care for it, and how to be a more knowledgeable double bass player.

The first section of this book reviews information that might be on the first few pages of your method book. Even if you know that information, spend a few moments reading this section to see if you can find something you did not yet learn. You will learn facts about the double bass that not many students will know.

You do not have to read this book in the order in which the chapters appear. Start at any chapter that may interest you, and then, as you progress, move around to the chapters related to your double bass studies.

NOTE: In the music world, the terms tailpiece, pegbox, and soundpost can also be written as two words. You might see them as tail piece, peg box, and sound post.

Note: The following explains a system used throughout all music studies called ***Scientific Pitch Notation***. This is a valuable tool that can serve you throughout your music career.

Scientific Pitch Notation helps you know exactly where a note is located on the staff without seeing the note in print. This system uses a combination of letters and numerals (alphanumeric) to tell you exactly where a note is in the entire range of notes. An example would be middle C, whose alphanumeric name is C4. The C one octave below middle C is C3. The C an octave above middle C is C5. The notes going up between these Cs keep the C's numeral until the next C is reached. Examples would be C4, D4, E4, F4, G4, A4, B4, C5, D5, etc. The figure below shows the alphanumeric symbol for all notes.

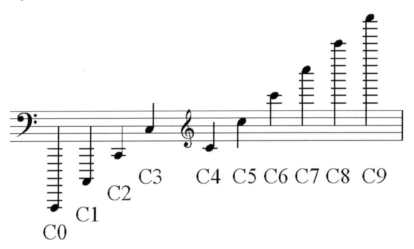

Chapter 1

What Are the Parts of My Double Bass, and How Do They Work?

Lesson One

Double Bass Parts

Let's begin by learning the names of some parts of your double bass. Locate the named parts on your double bass using the picture below as a guide.

Diagram compliments of https://gollihurmusic.com

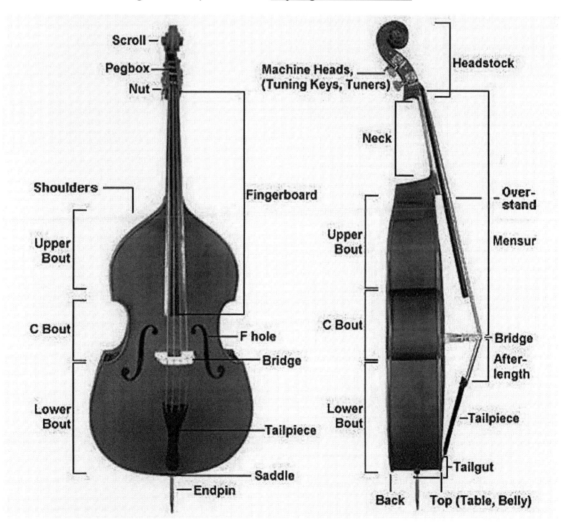

Here are some close-up pictures of the smaller parts shown above.

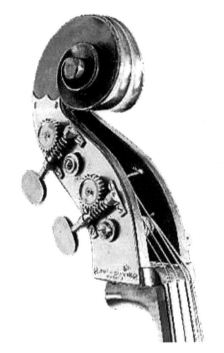

Headstock

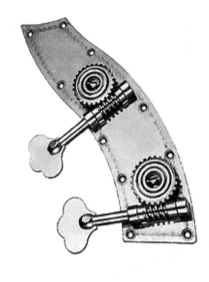

Machine Head (Tuning Keys)

Pegbox

Nut

Below are three different kinds of double bass bridges. The traditional bridge must be fitted to each instrument. The Aubert Self Adjusting feet bridge has feet that automatically rock back and forth to adjust to the shape of the instrument's top. The adjustable height bridge has a rotating screw on each foot that can adjust the bridge's height.

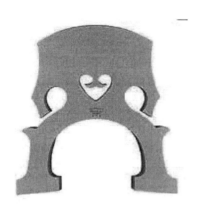

Traditional   **Aubert Self-Adjusting Feet**

Closed   **Raised**   **Parts**

Tailpiece

Tail gut

Saddle

Endpin

Next are the names of the parts that support the strings to produce sound.

1. strings
2. bridge
3. top
4. soundpost
   (inside)
5. back
6. bass bar
   (inside top)
7. sides
8. "ƒ" hole
9. purfling

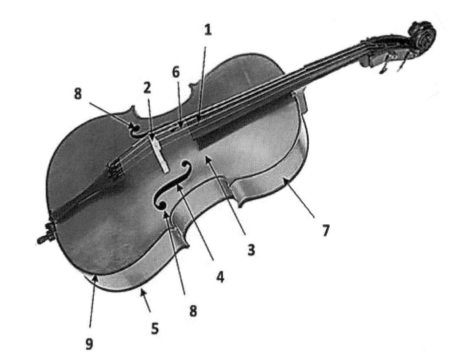

Let's look inside a double bass.

Supporting the top and back of your double bass are the following:

A. ribs and linings
B. top and bottom blocks
C. corner blocks
D. bass bar
E. soundpost

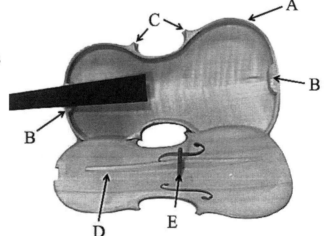

All the inside parts work together to strengthen the sound you hear as you bow or pluck a string.

Lesson Two

How Do the Parts Work?

The Bridge — The sound you produce when you pluck or bow a string travels to the feet of the bridge and then through to the top of your double bass.

"ƒ" Holes — "ƒ" holes are the f-shaped holes cut into the top of your double bass. There is one "ƒ" hole on each side of the bridge. These "ƒ" shaped openings let out the sound that is vibrating inside the body of the instrument.

The Soundpost— The soundpost is inside the body of your double bass. Look inside through the "ƒ" hole on the G string side. The soundpost is made of soft wood. It supports the top of your double bass and sends the high notes from the instrument's top to its back.

The Bass Bar —The bass bar is on the underside of the top of your double bass beneath the bridge foot on the E string side. The bass bar strengthens your instrument's top while carrying the lower notes throughout the instrument's top. You can see a bass bar by placing a dental mirror in the *"f"* hole on the E-string side of your instrument.

The combination of the bridge, soundpost and bass bar with the top and back produce the sound you hear when you bow or pluck a string.

The Sides and Back — The sides and back of your double bass hold the instrument together.

These parts are made of very strong maple wood. The strength is needed to support the pressure the tightened strings put on the top of your double bass. When all four strings are tuned, the pressure they put on the instrument equals about 70 pounds, the weight of a pile of almost 47 iPads.

Purfling — Two parallel strips of ebony, a dark hardwood, are inserted into the surface around the edge of the top and back of your double bass.

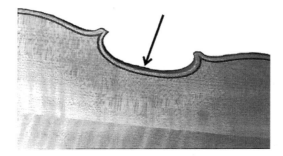

These two strips of wood are called purfling. They outline the area that will vibrate on the top and back of your double bass. They also add strength to the edges of the instrument's body.

Lesson Three

The Sound Voyage

Using the same picture where you learned the names of your double bass's parts, let's follow the trip sound makes throughout your instrument as you play.

When you bow or pluck a string (1)

its motion (vibration) is picked up by the bridge (2)

and sent to the top of the double bass(3).

That vibration travels to the soundpost (4)

which carries the vibration to the double bass back (5)

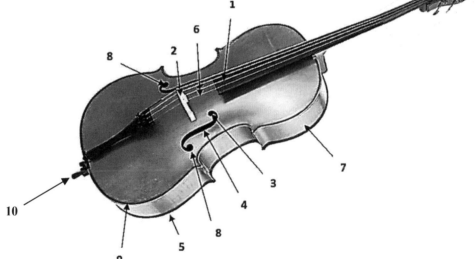

and is spread throughout the instrument's top by the bass bar (6).

The top and back of the double bass are supported by its sides (7).

The motion of all these parts sets the air inside the body into a pumping action that forces the sound out through the *"f"* holes (8).

The small wooden strips called purfling (9) around the edge of the double bass control sound vibration throughout the top and back and give strength to the edges.

The double bass rests on the endpin (10), which can be adjusted for height.

Lesson Four

Tuning Your Double Bass

The term pitch refers to how high or low a note is. To tune your double bass, you must hear the correct pitch for each string. The open strings are pictured below.

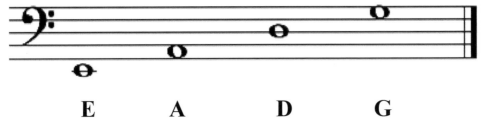

E   A   D   G

Note: The notes played on the double bass sound an octave lower than written, so the actual sound you will hear will be E1, A1, D2, and G2.

Tuning your double bass will be easy if you understand how the tuning mechanism works. The double bass has a post and gear system called a machine head, pictured below. Three views show the system on a bass headstock, a single outside view, and a combined outside/inside view.

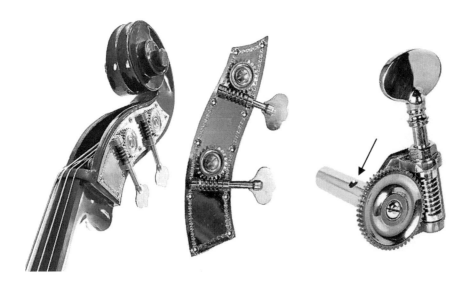

You can get the right sounds for E, A, D, and G from a piano, a pitch pipe, or a clip-on electronic tuner (pictured below). These are just some of the many different tuning aids you can use. (See chapter 4 on double bass accessories for more information on these devices).

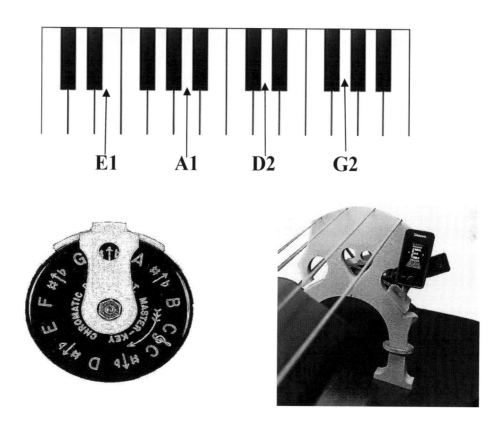

E1   A1   D2   G2

You can also Google _YouTube tuning a double bass,_ where you will find several videos that will help you do a perfect job of tuning.

The following is one of the recommended ways to tune your doube bass. As pictured above, it is best to have a clip-on tuner connected to your bridge.

1. Select the pitch you need (E, A, D, or G) for the string you are tuning.

2. Hold the instrument in a normal playing position.

3. Sound the pitch of the string you are tuning on the tuning device and try to fix that sound in your mind. Singing the pitch with the tuner will help.

4. When you have the pitch firmly fixed in your mind, pluck the string to be tuned.

5. While the string is sounding the note you have just plucked, read the clip-on tuner to see if the pitch is low or high. If it is low, turn the tuning key _slowly_ to the right, and the pitch will go up. If the pitch is too high, turn the tuning key to the left, and the pitch will go down.

6. While turning the tuning key slowly, continue plucking the string and listen to the pitch change. When it reaches the pitch you have in mind, stop. The string will be tuned.

7. When you feel you have reached the correct pitch, put your bass in the playing position and play each open string with your bow. As you play each note, check the pitch against your tuning device again and make the necessary adjustments. Sometimes, the tuning process will slightly change the pitch of the strings you have already tuned.

Lesson Five

Your Bow

The Bow — The double bass uses two kinds of bows with different frogs and holding positions. The French bow is Pictured below on top, and the butler or German bow is below it.

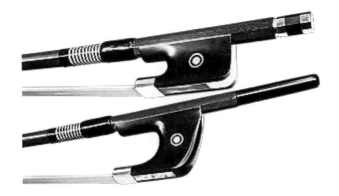

Holding the Bow — Using your method book, with your teacher's help, you have learned how to hold and use a French or German double bass bow.

The bow-hold section of www.stringbassonline.com shows bow-holding positions for both the French and German double bass bows. Although most teachers recommend a basic hand position, double bass players often modify that position to suit their individual hand structure and playing needs. As you play your instrument, you may inadvertently adjust your bow-holding position. If you establish a bow hold that works for you, consult your teacher to decide if you should keep that adjustment.

Now let's learn about the parts of a bow.

Bow Hair — A double bass bow is made up of about 300 hairs connected to a stick. The hair can be taken from a horse's tail or be manmade. Horsehair is the better choice, but some very good manmade (synthetic) bow hair is also in use.

Looking closely at bow hair, you will think it is smooth. But looking at bow hair under a microscope, you will be surprised to see that the surface is rough. The picture below shows magnified horsehair.

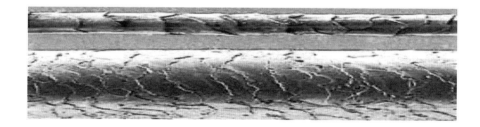

Bow Hair under a Microscope
Courtesy of bwlibys.blogspot.com

As you pass your bow over a string, this rough surface, along with the double bass rosin that you applied to the hair, catches on to the string causing it to vibrate and make a sound.

Bow Parts — The diagram below shows how the hair is connected to the bow stick.

The end of the bow hair (A) is wedged tightly into a box-shaped cutout called a mortise (B) at the tip of the bow.

The hair is held in place by a wooden, wedge-shaped plug (C) that is cut to exactly fit the space in the cutout box.

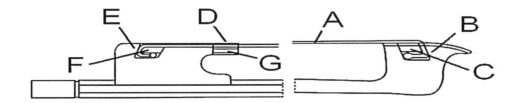

A metal band called a ferrule (D) is placed over the hair, which is carefully drawn along the bow, tied at the end, and forced into another box-shaped cutout in the frog. (E).

Another wooden wedge-shaped plug is placed into the box (F) to keep the hair in place.

Finally, a slide and a third wooden wedge are placed between the ferrule and the frog (G) to help spread the hairs and keep them in place.

Tightening and Loosening Bow Hair — You probably learned how to tighten and loosen your bow at your first lesson. Let's take a closer look at the bow parts you use when adjusting your bow hair.

These are pictures of the frog end of a German and French double bass bow.

This is a picture of an eyelet, the screw that fits into the eyelet, and a frog with the screw and eyelet.

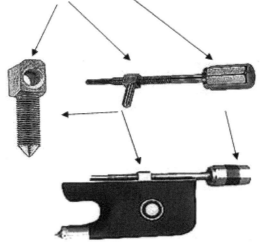

When you turn the screw, it moves in or out of the eyelet, which is attached to the frog. The eyelet pulls or pushes the frog back and forth. Turning the screw to the right will pull the frog back and tighten the bow hair. Turning the screw to the left will push the frog forward and loosen the bow hair.

Lesson Six

Changing Notes

The double bass has four strings that are tuned to E, A, D, and G. You can raise the pitch of each string by pressing the string to the fingerboard with the fingers of your left hand. Your teacher has taught you the correct position to use for fingering the notes. As you do so, keep an arch in your hand, and don't collapse the palm of your hand on the strings.

This is how it works:

You shorten its vibrating part when you press a finger on a string. Shorter strings produce higher sounds, and longer strings produce lower sounds. You learned in your lesson book how to finger the different notes starting with the first finger about 3 inches from the nut on any string. That is called first position. To be sure you have your finger in the right spot, set your tuning device to that note and check the pitch.

There are twelve positions on the double bass, seven positions, and five half positions.

Dr. Robin Deverich, the creator of the website www.stringbassonline, has consented to include the Advanced Fingering Chart 1st - 7th Positions.

Using the chart below as your guide, you will see that you are playing in:

1. ½ position when your first finger is one half step up from the open string.

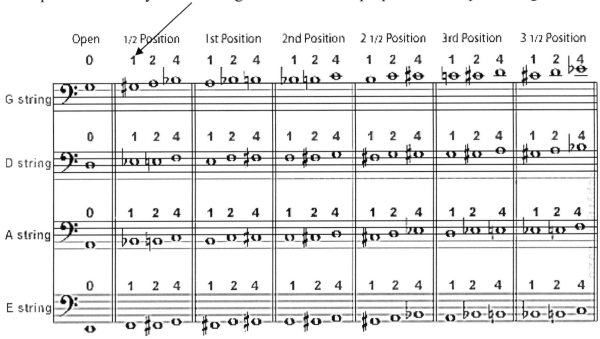

2. first position when your first finger is where your second finger was in half position.

3. second position when your first finger is where your second finger was in first position.

4. second ½ position is when your first finger is where your second finger was in second position.

5. third position when your first finger is where your second finger was in 2 ½ position.

6. third ½ position when your first finger is where your second finger was in third position.

7. fourth position is when your first finger is where your second finger was in 3 ½ position.

19

8. fifth position when your first finger is where your second finger was in fourth position.

9. fifth ½ position is when your first finger is where your second finger was in fifth position.

10. sixth position when your first finger is where your second finger was in fifth ½ position.

11. sixth ½ position when your first finger is where your second finger was in sixth position.

12. seventh position, when your first finger is where your second finger is where your second finger was in 6 ½ position.

Basic Double Bass Fingering Chart

To finger a particular note, press the string at the position noted on the chart using the finger indicated at the left.

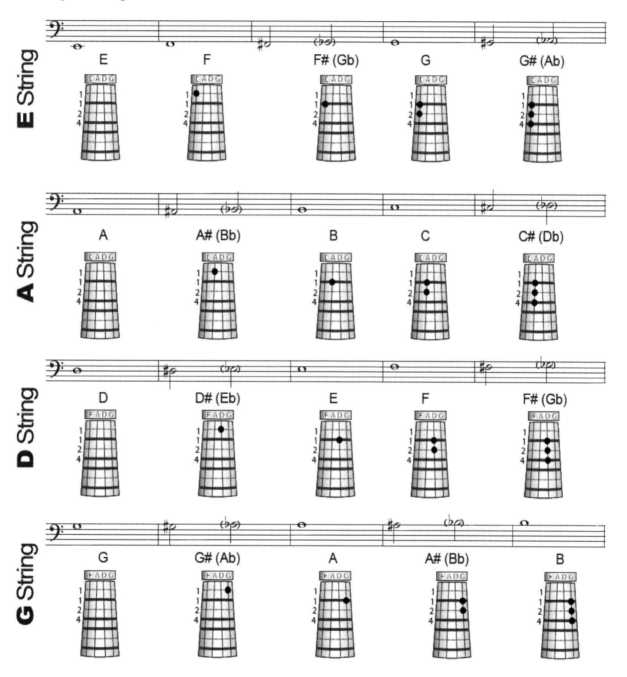

NOTES

Chapter 2

How Do I Care for My Double Bass Outfit?

Your double bass and bow need very special care because:

1. They are made of wood that can crack or break if dropped or treated roughly,

2. the wood can be damaged by extreme heat, cold, or very damp or dry air,

3. the wood has a fine finish that can be scratched or damaged by dirt and rosin dust.

Lesson One

Let's See How We Can Prevent These Mishaps

1. To avoid damage from having your double bass fall over, always place it on a double bass stand or its side on the floor.

2. Never put music or books in your double bass hard case. The case is made to fit the shape of your double bass and does not have extra space for other items. Soft cases usually have a pocket on the back for extra items and one on the front for the bow.

3. Store your double bass in your house where you would be comfortable, not in the attic, basement, or garage.

4. When traveling by car, keep the instrument in the car where the temperature is comfortable. Never leave the double bass in an unoccupied car. The double basses can become too hot or cold and can be stolen.

5. The finish on your double bass is probably varnish or some form of lacquer. These finishes can be easily scratched, so protect the finish from any items that may cause damage to the finish,

6. Wash your hands before you handle your double bass. Natural hand oil or other substances on your hands can damage the surface of your instrument.

7. Follow the instructions in lesson 2 on wiping the surfaces of your instrument and strings after each use. Rosin dust left on these surfaces can damage them.

8. When traveling with your double bass, on bus, train, or plane keep the instrument in the same location you occupy. A luggage compartment is not a good place for storage during travel. Keep the instrument as close to you as possible.

Lesson Two

Maintaining Your Double Bass Outfit

1. Wipe the surfaces of the instrument and the strings with a soft cotton cloth to remove any rosin dust, natural skin oils, and perspiration.

2. Wipe the bow stick and frog with the same cloth.

3. If your double bass or bow stick show signs of dirt or rosin that will not come off with the dry cloth, it is time to use a double bass polish, which can be bought in any music store or online. Ask your teacher what you should use for this problem. Be careful not to get polish on the bow hair.

Making Minor Adjustments

Adjusting the Bridge

(Ask your teacher to help you the first time you try this.)

Each time you tune your double bass, the strings move the bridge a tiny bit toward the fingerboard. To adjust your bridge:

1. Wrap your tailpiece in a soft cloth to prevent scratching the instrument's top should the bridge fall.

2. Loosen the strings just a bit.

3. Place the instrument on its back on a soft surface with the bridge facing up. Some possibilities are a soft rug, a table covered with bath towels, or even a bed.

4. Using the thumb and forefinger of each hand, grip the bridge at the middle of each side and move it back to its upright position.

5. Check the bridge feet to see if they are in perfect contact with the instrument's top.

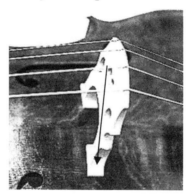

6. Re-tune the instrument (chapter 1).

Bridge Placement

The exact position of the bridge on your double bass is very important because the bridge carries the string's sound down to the top and then throughout the entire instrument.

To check your bridge's location — Look at the middle of your *"f"* holes, and you will see a notch on each side. The bridge feet should be in line with the notches on the bridge side of the *"f"* holes.

Lesson Three

Changing a String

The size of a double bass makes changing a string a bit more physical that doing so on other string instruments. If you follow the steps below, you will be successful. You will need a:

1. flat surface on which to lay the double bass on its back

2. some form of padding for that surface (your double bass carry bag works well)

3. #2 pencil,

4. towel or soft cloth to cover the tailpiece

5. double bass string winder

6. grade 0000 steel wool

7. linseed oil

8. strings

The Process

Note: It is best to remove and replace only two strings on one side and then do the same to the other side. Loosening all the strings at one time can cause the bridge to fall, the tailpiece to scratch the instrument's surface, and the soundpost to fall.

1. Prepare the flat surface by laying out the double bass bag or some other soft padding.

2. Lay the double bass on its back (bridge up) on that surface.

3. Using the string winder, unwind and remove the E string.

4. Do so on the A string.

5. Set the peg shaft hole facing down toward the nut, not facing you.

6. Using your #2 pencil, rub the graphite point on the slot in the nut and bridge where the string will rest. Doing so will lubricate the slot and lower friction when the string passes up and down as you tune.

7. Thread the new string through the tailpiece.

8. Put the top end of the string in the peg hole shaft from the top going down,

9. Draw about one-third of the fabric end of the string through the hole, and wrap the string around itself.

10. Using your string winder, wrap the string three times away from the pegbox cheek (side) and then cross over in the other direction to keep the E string in line with its slot in the nut. Do not let the string gather on the side of the pegbox.

11. Try to make this string-to-nut slot alignment on all strings.

12. As you remove each group of two strings, pass the steel wool lightly over the fingerboard to clean the surface. If the wood appears to dry, apply a light coat of linseed oil and then wipe clean.

13. Repeat the process for the other strings.

14. Tune the strings as you learned above, and then tune them again in a few hours, as the new strings will need to stretch and settle.

  This is an inside and outside view of the machine head. See the arrow where the strings go into the hole facing the nut.

Pegbox with strings properly aligned to meet the slot in the nut.

Lesson Four

Caring for Your Fine Tuners

If your double bass tailpiece is fitted with fine tuners, the bottom bar gets lower each time you turn the knob on your fine tuner to the right. When it reaches the bottom, turn it back to its original position and re-tune your double bass.

Lesson Five

Bow Care

1. Always keep your bow where you keep your double bass. They are safest in their case.

2. Do not leave your bow on a music stand or a chair. The bow can easily be knocked off the stand or be sat on if on a chair. Use a bow hook pictured chapter 4.

3. When preparing to use your bow, tighten your bow hair to the point where you feel the hairs are firm enough to produce the sound you want.

4. When your bow hair is tight, your bow stick should curve toward the hair. If it does not, show it to your teacher for advice.

5. When not in use, loosen the hair on your bow.

6. Never touch the bow hair with your fingers. The natural oil from your skin will soil the hairs, and the bow will not work well.

7. If a hair breaks, do not pull it off the bow. Cut it off at the frog and tip with scissors to avoid damage to the other hairs.

Cleaning Your Bow Hair

1. To clean your bow hair, moisten a soft cloth with isopropyl rubbing alcohol. With that cloth, wipe the hair in an up-and-down motion until it is clean. Do not let the alcohol touch the bow stick because the alcohol will damage the finish on the wood.

2. When the alcohol on the hair dries, gently run a comb up and down the hairs to loosen them. Then rosin your bow as usual. Ask your teacher about a product called the "Bow Hair Rejuvenation Kit" (p. 42), which is excellent for keeping your bow in playing condition.

3. When a bow is left in a case for a long time, you may find that the hairs are falling off the stick. This is caused by tiny insects called dermestids (bow bugs). If this happens, remove the bow from the case, cut off all the bow hair with a scissor, discard the hair and send the bow to a bow maker for rehairing.

4. Next, vacuum the case thoroughly, giving special care to the corners and edges. Then spray the case with an insecticide, and let the case remain open in a bright sunlit place for a few days.

Cleaning Your Bow Stick— Use a soft cloth to wipe the rosin dust from your bow stick after each use. If your bow stick is caked with dry rosin, use a double bass polish to clean the stick. Be extra careful not to get double bass polish on the bow hair.

Lesson Six

Case Care

Cleaning Your Double Bass Case — Keeping the inside and outside of your double bass case clean is important. The insides of hard cases are lined with a special material that will protect the double bass from damage. That material collects lint, rosin dust, and any other small matter that enters your case.

To care for the inside of your case, use a vacuum with a hose and pointed nozzle or hand vac and go at it. Be sure to get into all the corners and seams in the case.

The outside of hard double bass cases can be made of molded plastic, wood, or plastic covered with different materials. Molded plastic cases can be wiped with a damp cloth and, when dry, polished with a spray polish like Pledge. Fabric case cleaning depends on the fabric. Usually, this is canvas and can be wiped with a damp cloth (no soap) to remove any dirt or dust collected on the case cover.

Double basses and bows can last hundreds of years if properly cared for. The process is not hard to do, nor does it take much time. Make a habit of regularly going through the above-listed procedures, and your double bass might also be here a few hundred years from now.

Lesson Seven

Adjustments

Strings — The strings on your double bass rest on the nut (A), bridge (B), and tail-piece (C) (see arrows). Over time, those three areas can wear down. If you see string wear or wear on the slots where the string meets the nut, bridge, or tailpiece, ask your teacher's advice on how to deal with the problem.

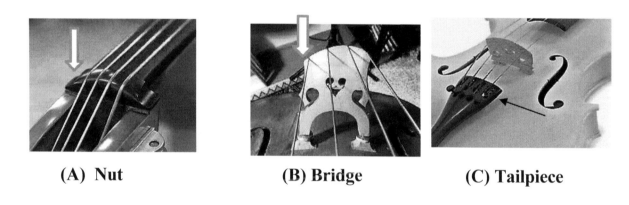

(A) Nut   (B) Bridge   (C) Tailpiece

If the string is wearing out, replace it. If one of those three parts shows wear, you will need a luthier (double bass maker) to replace the nut and the bridge. You can replace the tailpiece with your teacher's help.

Summary — Properly caring for your double bass, bow, and case will give the outfit a long life and allow it to serve you in the best way possible. These are the tools that you will use to make music. A good student with good equipment will make good music.

NOTES

Chapter 3

How Should I Plan My Practice Sessions?

I am sure you have heard that "practice makes perfect." Indeed, practice can make perfect, but only if you practice with understanding, patience, and the will to "get it right." Playing an exercise or musical selection many times over will not make it better unless you understand how the piece should sound and know what to do to make it sound that way. Playing a piece incorrectly repeatedly can result in your learning to play it wrong really well.

The following are some suggestions that will help you get the best results from your practice period:

1. Select a place in your home where you can practice without disturbing your family and where their daily life will not distract you from your work.

2. Pick a practice time that comfortably fits your daily study schedule. Try to use that same time each day for your studies.

3. Set a long-term general goal. In what ways do you want to improve your playing? Think of bowing, intonation, phrasing, dexterity (moving your fingers fast), and making beautiful music beautifully.

4. Have a plan for each practice period. What part of your long-term goal do you want to accomplish each period?

5. How long and how often should you practice? Daily practice is the best road to success. However, the amount of time you practice should vary with your goal. Shorter daily practice periods produce better results than less frequent long sessions.

6. After you have planned your goal and begun to practice, you will decide on the amount of time and how often practice will be necessary to achieve each target.

7. Discuss your plans with your teacher, who will be able to help you make the plan and reach your goal. The time you spend practicing is not as important as what you accomplish during your practice.

8. Equipment – It is important that you have all the equipment necessary to have a successful practice period. Your equipment should include a music stand, metronome, a stool if you plan to sit, rosin, a cleaning cloth, and anything else you need to be comfortable.

The Process

1. Begin your practice period with careful tuning of your double bass. Use whatever apps or tuning devices you feel will be best for you.

2. Warm up, starting with simple scales in first position using quarter notes. Play slowly and listen. Are you playing in tune?

3. After you are sure that you have the quarter note scales down, add rhythmic patterns of your own creation to those same scales. Listen carefully to intonation as you play. Playing in tune is a must.

4. As you advance, you can expand the warmup material to include exercises and any other music you like.

5. Follow your warmup by playing a tune that you like. Enjoy the music.

6. Improvisation is fun. Make up your own tune or try to play a tune "by ear." No need for printed music here.

7. Now, start practicing the material your teacher assigned in your last lesson. Follow the instructions carefully. Listen to yourself, sing the music before you play it, be sure you are playing in tune, and feel the rhythm.

8. Record yourself on your mobile phone as you play. Then listen to the recording and be very critical of your intonation, phrasing, and general musicianship.

9. Did you like what you heard? If your answer is yes – great! If it is no, think of what you did not like. Figure out how you can make it better. Then, make it better.

10. Check again to be sure you are playing in tune, using proper phrasing, and bowing. Are you keeping a proper playing position?

Apps and Your Mobil Phone

You can search for "apps for double bass practice and tuning using your mobile phone or computer. You will find many "apps" that are free and will help you tune and practice better. Some sites also have free music that you can print. Others show playing techniques and play-a-long sessions where you join with others to play double bass music. Use the same search on YouTube, and you will find many sites you will enjoy watching while learning about playing your double bass.

The following are just a few of the many apps you can find on your mobile phone or computer.

Best Double Bass Apps for Mobile Phones
Double Bass Notes App
Play Along Double Bass App
Play Along Double Bass App Android
Free Double Bass Music

Double Bass App for Android
Double Bass tuner App
Free Online Double Bass Tuner
Metronome
www.stringbassonline.com

NOTES

Chapter 4

What Items (Accessories) Will I Need to Help Me Play My Double Bass?

An accessory is something that will help you use your double bass but is not part of a basic double bass outfit. The descriptions and pictures of accessories below are just some of these items. You can find hundreds more on Google.

Rosin — Rosin, made from tree sap (resin), is used to make the hair on your bow sticky. This makes the hair grip the string as you bow to produce sound.

Rosin comes in amber (yellow) shades, from light to dark. Prices range from 99 cents to $35. and in some "very special" cases, even more. If you are a beginning student, start with the least expensive rosin available. It will work fine until your teacher recommends a change or you feel you need something different. Be sure to use double bass rosin, specially made for your double bass bow.

Rosin can have different degrees of hardness and color. Hard rosin, usually light amber, gives a dry powdery result. Its gripping power is lighter and best for smaller instruments. Soft rosin, darker in color, has a stickier texture and provides increased gripping power for the bow hair. This greater gripping power will produce a stronger sound. Double bass rosin is usually softer.

.

Tuning Forks — The tuning fork is the most basic device used to hear a pitch. Tuning forks are U-shaped and made of metal with a handle at the base of the U.

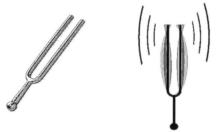

Hold a tuning fork by the handle and strike the tines (prongs) on a hard surface. The tines will vibrate. Then touch the stem to a hard surface, and you will hear the tone (pitch) caused by the vibrations. You can get a tuning fork for any pitch, but A 440 (440 vibrations per second) is the pitch A you would use to tune your A string.

Pitch Pipes — Pitch pipes are a necessary accessory for any double bass player. The simplest pitch pipe is made with four small pipes joined together. Each pipe is tuned to match the pitch of one string on the double bass. The pitches from low to high for the double bass are E, A, D, and G. You blow gently into the correct pipe to hear the pitch you need to tune a string. The picture on the right shows a pitch pipe with the four notes of the double bass strings.

A chromatic pitch pipe is round and has a marked opening for every pitch, including the scale's sharps and flats (chromatics). The notes start at C and progress in half steps up to the next C in the scale. You can pick any note, slide the white marker to that note's position on the pitch pipe, blow into that hole, and hear your chosen pitch.

Electronic Tuners —There are several kinds of electronic tuners. The simpler type produces the four pitches of the open strings for your double bass. Other models have all the notes. You select the pitch needed, press the correct button, and you will hear the pitch.

A more advanced tuner has a screen that shows an image of the pitch being sounded. When you bow or pluck a string, a needle on a screen will tell you if the sound is up (sharp), down (flat), or spot-on the pitch you want. You can then tune the string up or down until the correct pitch is reached.

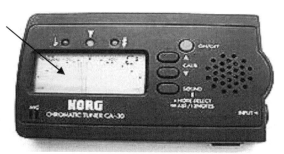

Clip-on tuners are very convenient because you can read the results as you play the note needed. Below is pictured one of many available clipped on a bridge.

Apps or Applications — Apps and websites on tuning can be found on your mobile phone, iPad, and computer. If you use one of these, try not to be distracted by using your practice time to try the technology. Amazon.com shows five pages, each with about fifteen different tuners for a total of seventy-five tuners of all kinds now on the market.

Fine tuners — Double bass tailpieces (pictured below) can be fitted with fine tuners. Having such a tailpiece on your instrument is a convenience that makes adjusting the pitch on your strings easier and more accurate.

Bow Hair Rejuvenation Kit — To remove rosin buildup and dirt from handling and the environment, use the ***Bow Hair Rejuvenation Kit***. In the kit, you will find a liquid bow-cleaning solvent, a cloth with which to apply the solvent, a comb to straighten out the hairs after the solvent dries, and a liquid rosin solution to apply to the hair at the end of the cleaning process. Follow the instructions. It works.

Rock Stop — AKA endpin stopper, endpin anchor rest holder, and double bass floor protector is a device used to prevent double bass endpins from slipping or damaging the floor. Below is pictured a:

Wolf Super Endpin Stop   **Rock Stop**   **Endpin Anchor**

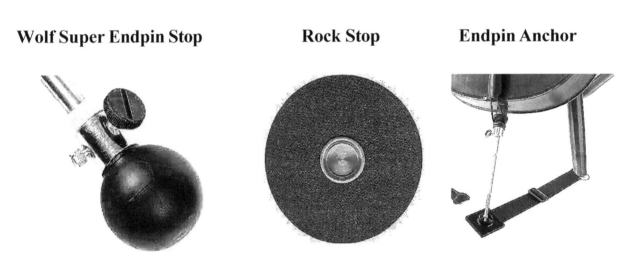

There are many more.

Strings — As you progress in your studies, you will want to learn more about the different kinds of double bass strings and how they can improve the sound of your instrument. A computer search shows fifty-seven different brands of double bass strings. These strings can be made of gut, steel, perlon (plastic fiber), nylon, silk, chromium/steel, silver, and gold. Each type of string produces a different sound and can change the tone quality of your instrument.

Steel or Steel Core strings are the strongest, produce the brightest sound, stay in tune longer, and are best used by beginning players.

Gut Strings produce a mellow sound but react to temperature and humidity changes. This can cause problems with keeping your double bass in tune. Gut strings tend to break more easily than steel strings.

Gut Core strings are gut strings that are wound with silver or aluminum. These produce a fuller sound than plain gut and are stronger.

Synthetic Core strings are made with nylon or another manmade material as a core. These strings are stronger than gut, do not react greatly to temperature and humidity changes, and stay in tune longer.

Strings are made with a ball, loop, or knot end to connect to the tailpiece. The loop and ball ends are usually found on most strings, whereas the knot end is used for gut strings without windings.

String Winder — A string winder turns changing a string on a double bass from a tedious task to a simple job. Hook the slot on the winder to the tuning machine key and wind away.

Mutes — A mute changes tone, quality, and volume. Mutes can be made of wire with a plastic arch, a rubber disc, five rubber prongs, or three wooden prongs. Below are four examples of mutes for a double bass.

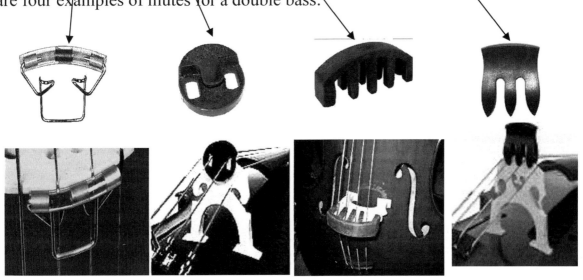

Wolf Tone Eliminator — A wolf tone is a howling-like sound that can occur on some basses when playing certain notes (usually in the area of Bb). Placing a wolf tone eliminator on the offending string below the bridge will eliminate that sound. Below are pictured two of the most popular wolf tone eliminators.

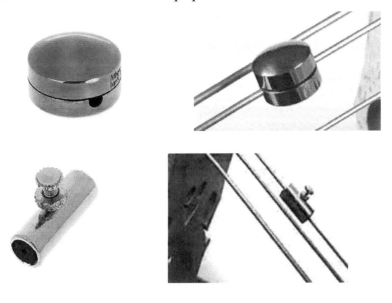

Double Bass Stands — Between use, it is best to have your double bass on a stand instead of laying it on its side on the floor, which could damage the edges of the instrument. Below are pictured four different kinds of stands. Each positions the instrument differently. There are many variations of those types.

Double bass Cases — Double bass cases made of fabric, usually canvas, are called soft cases or gig bags. A basic gig bag will have a simple carrying strap on its side, a pocket for the bow on the front, and an accessories pocket on the back.

Hard cases are usually made of plastic with a felt inside coating. Either type will also be available with a padded lining to offer greater protection for your double bass.

Below are examples of the back and front of a soft case and the outside and inside of a hard case

Traveling with a double bass can be challenging for you and the instrument. Below is one style case made to protect the instrument and facilitate movement.

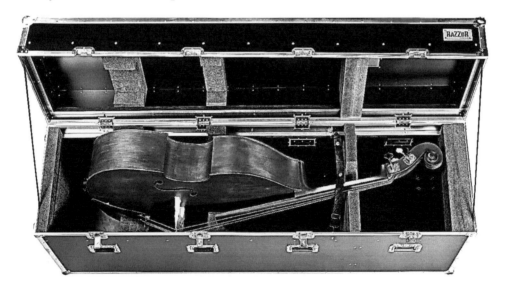

Bow Cases — If you use a bass bag for storage and travel, your bow will be in a pocket, usually in the front. That bow storage offers little protection. A safe way for bow storage and transportation is a bow case, as pictured below. Note the accessory bag on the front cover.

Bass Bow Quiver — A bass bow quiver is the best bet for safe bow storage between playing sets. They are available in many designs and are made of different materials.

Bass Transport Device — A double bass can weigh as much as twenty-five pounds. There are many devices designed to ease the movement of the instrument. The pictures below show a sample of each possible design.

Beach Rolly

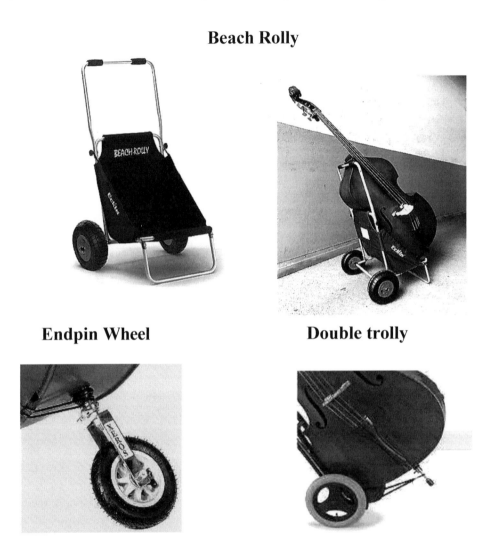

Endpin Wheel   **Double trolly**

Bow Hook — To have your bow immediately available while playing pizzicato, a bow hook like the ones pictured below will do the job. The hook on the left attaches to the shaft of your music stand, and the other can clip onto the music tray.

Hygrometers — A hygrometer measures the humidity level in a double bass case. If a hygrometer shows a dry climate, you will need to place a humidifier in the case. Below are two of many kinds of hygrometers.

Digital   **Analog**

Humidifiers — A Dampit humidifier is a perforated rubber tube filled with an absorbent material that holds water. When your double bass is not in use, insert the Dampit tube soaked in water into the instrument's body through the F hole. Remove the Dampit when you use the instrument. A humidity-measuring color chart that shows the humidity level is included with the Dampit kit.

Search "Double bass case humidifiers" on Google Images, and you will find more of these products.

Double Bass Stools — Because you play your bass standing up for a long period of practice or performance can be tiring, the music industry offers a variety of stools designed to accommodate your playing position. Below are just three examples of the many designs available. From left to right, the first is fully adjustable with a back but not very portable. The second is bike seat shaped and also adjustable for height. The third type can be folded for easy travel. There are many more.

Music Stands — Music stands are made in three designs. There are stands that fold, those that are rigid or non-folding, and tabletop stands.

A folding stand or sheet music stand is very useful for a beginning student. It is lightweight, totally portable, and very inexpensive. Folding stands can also be purchased with a carrying case for even more convenient portability. These stands can easily be knocked over, and the lightweight parts can be bent out of shape.

A rigid design stand sometimes referred to as a concert, stage, or orchestra music stand, is not easy to carry, is quite heavy, and is made to be used in one place. It is more expensive than the folding stand but is very stable, able to hold a large amount of music, and is strong. A rigid stand can cost two to four times that of a folding stand.

A small tabletop stand does not have legs and is lightweight and inexpensive. It can be placed on any stable surface and allows complete flexibility. Below are three models of tabletop stands: the first a decorative model, the second a folding design, and the third a concert style.

Double Bass Polish — Double basses require routine care. Using the correct polish is important to keep the instrument in good condition. Below are three of the many products available for you to use when caring for your bass. The kits include a cleaning agent and a polish.

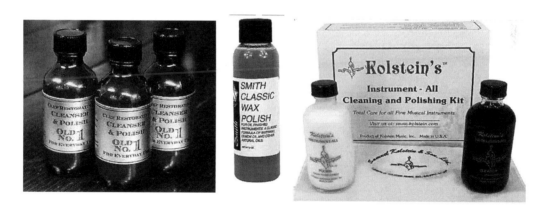

Double Bass Bib — As you play your double bass, it comes in contact with your body, causing wear to the instrument's finish. A bib in the right location on the instrument will prevent that wear. Below are three kinds of bibs in place on an instrument.

  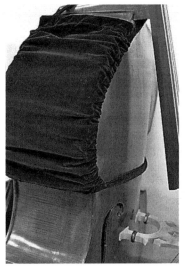

Summary This chapter showed some accessories that can make your double bass study easier. To see more accessories google "double bass accessories," and you might spend the day looking through the results.

Chapter 5

How Are Double Basses Made?

Understanding how your double bass is made helps you better understand how it works and how to play it. Double basses can be custom-made, handmade, or factory-made.

Custom Made means handmade by a luthier (string instrument maker) for a certain customer. This is how it is done:

1. The luthier chooses the woods to be used. These may come from different parts of the world because the same kind of wood grown in different climates will develop differently.
    A. Maple wood is used for a double bass's back, sides, and neck.
    B. Spruce wood is used to make the top.
    C. Ebony or rosewood is used for the fingerboard, pegs, purfling, and trim.

Other kinds of wood and manmade products, such as plastic and metal, can be used as substitutes; however, maple, spruce, rosewood, and ebony are the best materials for making a good double bass.

2. The next step is to design the instrument. Often, the luthier will begin by using a copy of the double basses of the great luthiers you will read about in chapter 6, such as da Salo, Guarneri, and Amati. These models can then be adjusted to suit the plan for the new double bass to be built.

3. When the wood and design patterns are decided upon, the luthier carves, shapes and molds the parts to fit the design selected.

4. The double bass is assembled, stained, varnished, and hand-rubbed.

5. The luthier fits the instrument with pegs, a tailpiece, a bridge, and strings.

Handmade double basses can be made by more than one luthier within a shop. Each part is made by a luthier who specializes in making that part. The handmade parts are then assembled by another maker and set up by yet another. The instrument is still handmade but by more than one pair of hands.

Factory-made double basses are made of parts carved by computer-guided woodworking machines. The parts are put together by hand.

The Process

Step 1 – Establishing the Pattern — The luthier will decide on the double bass's size and shape. As mentioned before, usually, it will be a copy of one of the great masters such as da Salo, Amati, or any other master instrument makers you will read about in Chapter 6.

Step 2 – Selecting the Materials — The major parts of the double bass will be spruce for the top, maple for the sides, back, and neck, and ebony or rosewood for the fingerboard and trim. Small inner parts called blocks and linings are often made of willow. It is also time to select the type of machine heads as described in chapter one to be used on this instrument.

Definition: The "grain" is the pattern or shape of the fibers you see in a piece of wood.

A double bass made from wood with an even grain will produce a better sound than one with an uneven grain. If the luthier makes a one-piece top or back, the grain will spread out as it goes across the piece. If a triangle cut, which you will see on the next page, is used to make a two-piece top or back, the wood is taken from a smaller section of the tree, and the grain will be closer.

Step 3 – Cutting the Wood — There are two ways wood can be cut to make a double bass's top and back (plates). For a two-piece top or back:

1. A V-shaped block is cut out of a slice of a tree stump.

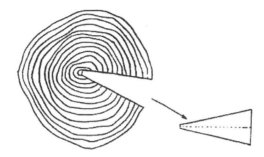

=]2. The V-shape is cut down its center to form two separate triangular pieces.

Step 4 – Joining the Cuts — The two pieces are joined together "book matched" with hide glue, a glue that can be melted with warm water. The matched pieces of the two-piece top or back are placed in a clamp to dry. When the glue is dry, the matched pieces will form one piece. Below are pictures of wood being "book matched," glued together, and drying in a clamp.

When the two pieces that have become one are removed from the clamp, an outline of a double bass's back is traced onto that piece, and the wood is cut following the outline. The final result is a two-piece back, shown below.

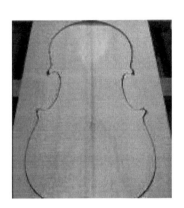  

If the luthier decides on a one-piece top or back:

1. A large layer of wood to make an entire back or top is cut from a tree stump.

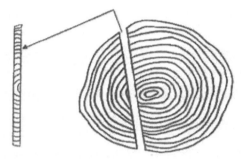

2. That wood slice is used to make a top or back without a seam in the middle.

Definition: The term "bout" is used to identify the three sections of a double bass body. The upper third is called the upper bout, the middle section is called the C bout, and the lower third is called the lower bout.

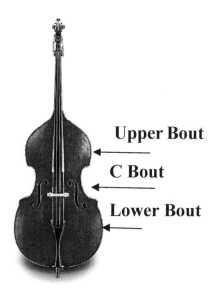

Upper Bout

C Bout

Lower Bout

Step 5 – The Mold — A mold is a double bass-shaped wooden form, which the luthier uses as a base for building the first parts of the instrument.

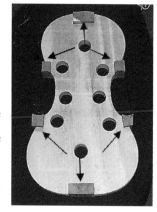

The luthier will place six wooden blocks (arrows) on the mold to act as anchors for the instrument's sides or ribs. One (corner) block is placed in each of the four corners of the C bouts, and a fifth and sixth (end) block is placed at the mold's upper and lower end.

Step 6 – The Ribs — A double bass's ribs (sides) are thin strips of maple wood. To create the ribs, the luthier wets thin wood strips to make them bend more easily. The strips are then heated, bent to shape, and glued onto the six corner blocks shown here.

Step 7 - The Linings — After the ribs have been glued to the blocks and the glue is dry, thin strips of wood called linings are glued inside the edge of the ribs. The linings support the ribs after they are removed from the mold.

Step 8 – Carving the Plates — In step 4, "joining the cuts," the top and back were rough cut. These must be carved into the shapes that will produce the best possible sound.

Step 9 – Purfling — Purfling is a thin, double strip of wood that is set into the edge of the top and back of a double bass. Purfling strengthens the instrument's edges and controls the vibrations traveling through the wood.

The picture below shows a luthier marking a groove (A), cutting a groove (B), and the finished product with the purfling installed (C).

A	B	C

Step 10 – Tuning the Plates (Top and Back) — It is now time for the luthier to carve the wood of the top and back of the double bass so they will vibrate to produce the best sound for that instrument. There are two ways to decide how much and where to remove wood from the two plates.

Originally it was done by the luthier tapping the plate and listening to the sound the tapping produces. Using the tapping method, the luthier taps on the plate in different places. This will produce "tap tones," which are actual pitches showing the experienced luthier how much wood should be shaved from different areas of the plate to get the best sound.

In 1787 Ernest Chladni (pronounced klad-nee), known as the father of acoustics (the study of sound), discovered that if you run a bow along the edge of a plate (top or back) held tightly in a clamp and sprinkled with glitter, the plate will vibrate. The glitter will move into certain patterns. The pattern of the glitter will show where vibration occurs and where to carve and not carve away some more wood. These patterns were called Chladni patterns. Below are two examples of Chladni patterns.

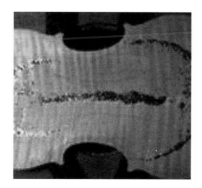 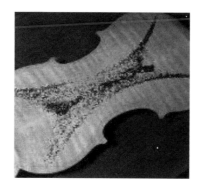

Step 11 – "ƒ" Holes — The shape and size of the "ƒ" holes or sound holes are important parts of the sound-producing system. A luthier can greatly improve a double bass's sound by the way the "ƒ" holes are cut. If the holes' size, shape, and distance are properly designed, the double bass's sound will be greatly improved. "ƒ" holes must be at least large enough to allow a soundpost to pass through later in the making process.

To make the *"f"* holes, the luthier marks the shape on the double bass's top plate and drills guide holes in places that outline the pattern of the *"f"* hole'. A jeweler's saw is used to make the cuts. The job is finished with a series of very sharp knives.

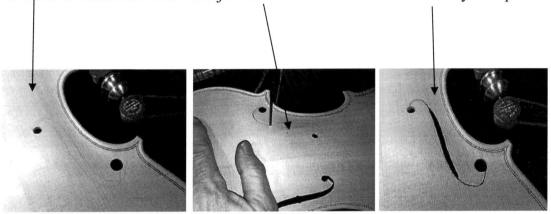

Step 12 - The Bass Bar — As you read in chapter 1, the bass bar is a strip of wood attached to the underside of the top plate. This strip strengthens the plate while spreading the lower pitches throughout that area. The bass bar is glued in place.

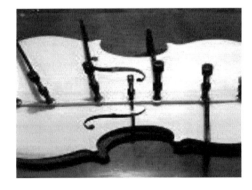

The clamps are removed when the glue is dry, and the luthier does another plate tuning, as described in step 10 above.

Step 13 – The Neck and Scroll — The neck and scroll are carved from one piece of hard wood (usually maple). The luthier draws an outline of the scroll on a wood block. A hand or electric saw is used to cut out the shape.

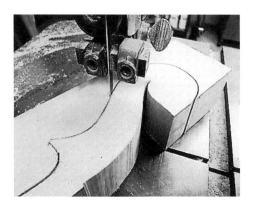 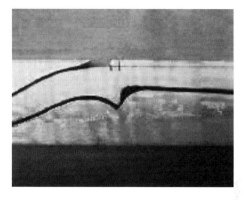

The location for the peg holes is marked on the cutout.

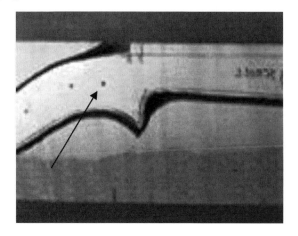

Step 14 – Peg Holes — Peg holes are drilled into the pegbox.

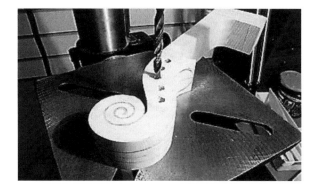

When those steps are completed, sharp knives and files are used to shape the neck.

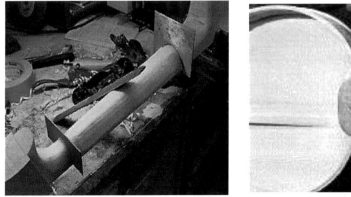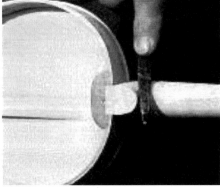

Step 15 – The Scroll — It is time to carve the scroll. This is done using several different saws, scrapers, and carving knives.

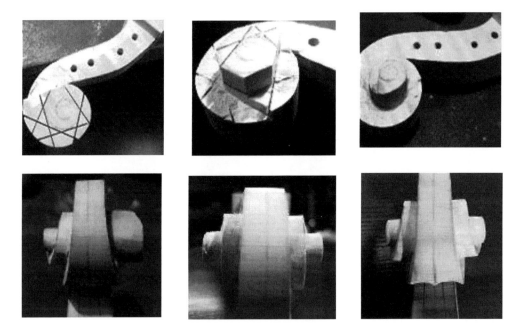

Step 16 – Carving the Pegbox — The pegbox is the space for the pegs with wound strings. The pegbox sides (called cheeks) are marked on the woodblock, and then the luthier uses a drill and chisel to remove the wood.

Step 17— Finishing the Pegbox — When the extra wood is removed, the luthier switches to sharp carving tools such as gouges to carve out the remaining wood to form the pegbox shape and size.

This part of the neck is ready to be attached to the instrument's body.

Step 18 – Fitting the Neck to the Body — The neck must be perfectly aligned with the body. The strings will travel from the pegbox over the nut, the fingerboard, and the bridge to end at the tailpiece. A mortise (opening) is cut into the top block to fit the base of the neck, which is then glued in place.

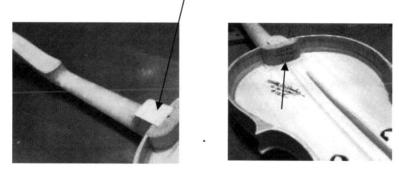

With the neck in place and the glue dry, the backplate is glued onto the ribs.

Step 19 — The Set up — A fingerboard is glued in place

 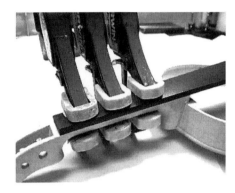

The nut and saddle are cut, finished, and glued in place.

Nut   **Saddle**

A bridge is cut to shape.

The soundpost is cut and put in place.

It is time to select and install tuning machine heads.

An endpin, tailgut, and tailpiece are fitted and installed at the bottom of the instrument

Without a varnish finish, the double bass is ready to be strung and tried for sound. The instrument has now been set up "in the white" (without a finish) for the first trial playing. At this time, the luthier will make any adjustments needed to improve the sound produced by this new double bass.

Step 20 — The Finish — The coating put on the raw wood of the double bass after it is complete is called the "finish." The five steps used to finish a double bass are:

1. the preparation of the wood,

2. putting on the first (ground) coat of wood treatment on the raw wood,

3. coloring the wood,

4. putting on a protective coating, and finally,

5. polishing the double bass.

A. Preparation — To prepare the raw wood, the luthier starts by wetting the wood's surface to swell the grain. The wood is then sanded and scraped until the luthier is satisfied with the appearance of the raw (unfinished) wood.

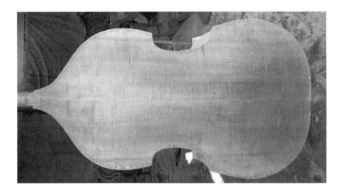

B. Ground Coat — A ground coat is a liquid sealer that will prepare raw wood to receive color and a finishing product. The ground will fill the pores and cover any spots in the wood. The result will be a smooth surface on which to apply the next step in the finishing process.

Heinrich Krutz, Luthier

C. Color —The luthier chooses and applies color to the double bass. The color may be wiped on with a cloth, sprayed, or brushed on.

D. Finishing Coat — The finishing coat will most often be varnish. Most luthiers agree that several coats with a fine sanding between each coat usually have the best results.

E. Polishing — When the varnish is dry, the luthier might improve the finish with hand polishing using any combination of oils, bees' wax, pumice, rotten-stone, and turpentine.

Summary — And so, another handmade double bass is born. With proper care, it can live for centuries. In the hands of professionals, it will provide the world with millions of notes that, when properly combined, will become music.

In the next chapter, you will read about the first person who plucked the string that made the sound that began the process that led to the double bass. What a wonder! Thank you, luthiers of the world, both past, and present, for your contributions to our musical joy.

Chapter 6

What Is the History of the Double bass?

It is difficult to put a date on the invention of the double bass. Rather than being invented, it probably evolved from a gradual series of changes to the viola da gamba to satisfy the needs of the musicians of the time. As the art of making string instruments grew and the needs of instrumentalists expanded, so did the instruments' size to produce lower sounds.

By the early 1500s, viols grew in size to the point where they were as big as their players. In about 1542, the Venetian Silvestro Ganassi built a viola da gamba large enough to be considered the predecessor to the double bass. The instrument had the sloping shoulders of today's double bass, with six strings covering a range from D2 to D4.

Let's look at some of these "before-the-double bass" instruments and see how they developed into the double bass we now know.

Lesson One

Plucked Instruments

The Kantele — The kantele is probably one of the earliest plucked instruments. It dates back several thousand years to the European countries that border the Baltic sea. The kantele was used to accompany singing and was not a solo instrument.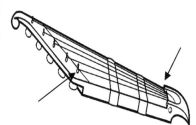

The strings on the kantele were stretched across the instrument's body, starting at the tuning pins and ending at a crossbar. Because there was no bridge or nut, the sound was like a bell. The strings were tuned to either a major or minor scale. The kantele was placed on a flat surface or on the player's lap, where it could be strummed or plucked with the fingers or a guitar-like pick called a plectrum.

The "U" Shaped Lyre — The picture on the right is a "U" shaped lyre. Notice the shape of the instrument, starting from the two arms at the top that forms a "U." Look at the body, and you will see the strings traveling over a bridge past a sound hole on either side of the bridge and attached to a tailpiece.

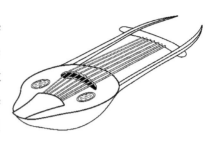

There is no fingerboard. The different pitches came from the thickness and tightness of the string. Look at your double bass, and you will see the same idea. Your G string is the thinnest and, as such, the highest-pitched. Your D string is next in thickness and is lower-pitched than the G string. The A and E strings follow that pattern. As you can see by the instrument's shape, it would not be possible to bow the strings. The strings had to be plucked.

The Lute — At the top, the lute has a pegbox and tuning pegs attached to strings that travel over the nut. The lute has frets (metal strips) on the fingerboard, similar to those found on a guitar. Also, note that the strings are connected directly to the bridge instead of passing over a bridge, as do those on your double bass. The back of the lute body was made of strips of wood instead of one or two pieces of wood that make up the back of a double bass.

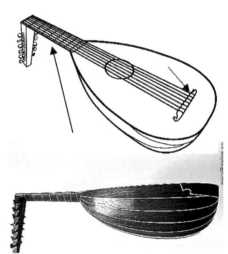

The Zither — Zither is a name for string instruments with strings stretched across a soundboard. A zither is played on a flat surface or the player's lap.

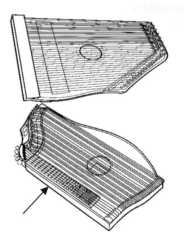

This instrument was very popular because it was easy to make and play. Because of this popularity, several different designs were developed. On the top right, you see an early zither with no fingerboard. The bottom right shows a zither with a fretted fingerboard under only five strings.

Timeline — The following timeline shows some of the early plucked instruments that might have appeared throughout history and what is probably one of the first bowed instruments.

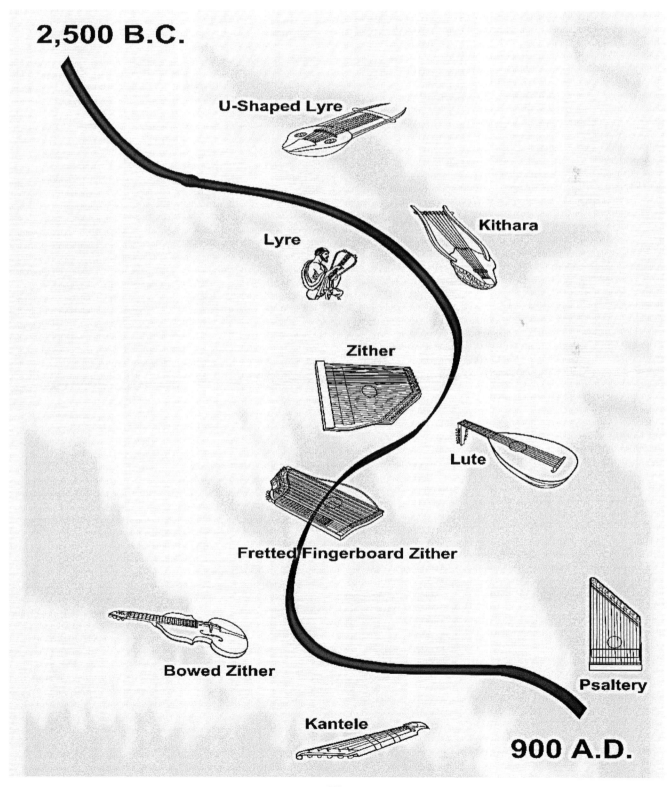

2,500 B.C.

U-Shaped Lyre

Kithara

Lyre

Zither

Lute

Fretted Fingerboard Zither

Bowed Zither

Psaltery

Kantele

900 A.D.

Lesson Two

Early Bowed Instruments

The Bowed Zither — The bowed zither arrives. Does it look familiar? Yes, we finally begin to see the shape of your double bass appear. The zither has a body shape that will allow a bow to pass over the strings, *"f"* holes on either side of the bridge, four pegs different from those on your double bass, and a fingerboard but with frets like a guitar.

At some point in history, musicians began understanding that by rubbing a tacky stick or chord across a string, they were producing a richer sound than plucking the string. And so began the early but not yet double bass-like bowed instruments.

In about 900 A.D., instruments with a body, fingerboard, pegbox, and tunable strings began to appear. Let's look at some of these instruments to see if we can find more signs of a double bass developing.

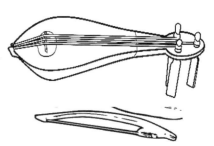

The Rebab — The rebab was an African bowed string instrument. The rebab was usually constructed with a pear-shaped body hollowed out from a block of wood. A thin sheet of wood or animal hide was then attached to the hollowed-out section to act as a top. Unlike the modern double bass, the fingerboard was part of the body instead of a separate piece attached to the instrument.

Rebabs usually had two or three strings that were played with a bow. As far back as the 8th Century, the rebab was played in North Africa, the Middle East, and Europe.

The Spike Fiddle — Another form of a rebab, a spike fiddle, had a round body. The neck was a round pole supporting the strings and extending down through the body to form an endpin. The player held the spike fiddle upright, resting it on the ground as you hold your double bass

The Rebec — The rebec existed in Europe during the 15th and 16th centuries. The rebec is like a rebab except for the body. The body of the rebec was made from the dried shell of a plant. This shell is called a gourd.

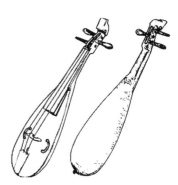

Up to now, most string instrument fingerboards were part of the instrument's body. Like the double bass, the rebec's fingerboard was made separately and then attached to the instrument's body.

The Vielle — The vielle appeared in France during the Medieval period from the thirteenth to the fifteenth Century. This instrument was closer in design to the modern double bass. Rather than having a gourd-shaped body, as did the rebec, the vielle's body was constructed like your double bass with a wider upper and lower section (bout) and a narrower midsection. This midsection allowed a player to use a bow more easily.

The vielle had a flat pegbox with the pegs on top of the pegbox facing upward. The vielle had five strings.

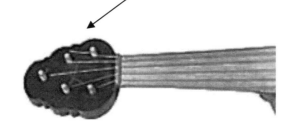

The timeline below shows the second phase in the evolution of string instruments.

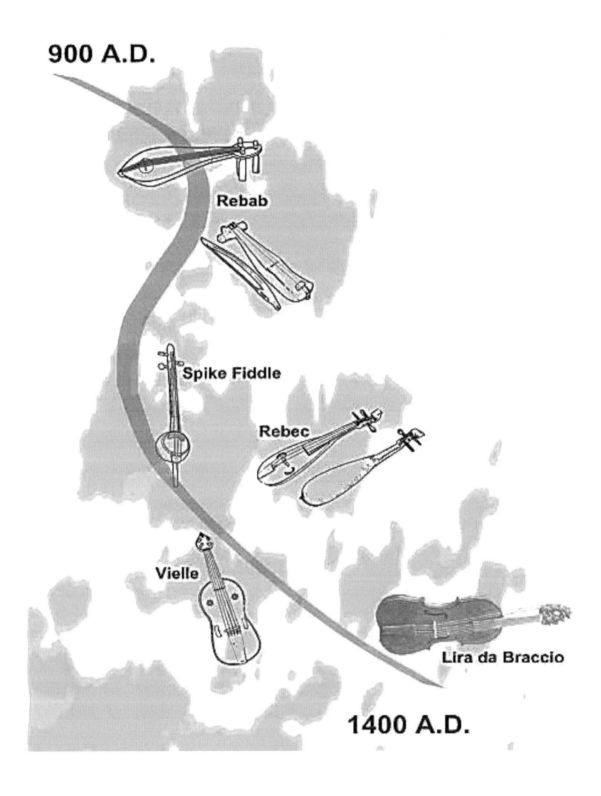

900 A.D.

Rebab

Spike Fiddle

Rebec

Vielle

Lira da Braccio

1400 A.D.

Lesson Three

The Birth of the Double bass

The Lira da Braccio (Lire of the Arm) — Following the vielle was the lira da braccio (Italian for lire of the arm) which first appeared in Italy. This was a bowed string instrument resembling a viola but with a wider fingerboard.

The lira da braccio could have as many as seven strings. Four were tuned to E, A, D, and G over a fingerboard, as are those of your double bass. Another low D string was placed over the fingerboard, and two other strings ran along the side of the fingerboard.

The tuning pegs on the lira da braccio were installed on the top of a leaf-shaped pegbox instead of on the sides as on your double bass. The picture above is of a lira da braccio in the Kunsthistorisches Museum, Musikinstrumente, Vienna, Austria.

The instrument was difficult to play because of the number of strings used to play melody and chords simultaneously. This led musicians to look at a larger instrument called the cello, one step closer to the double bass.

The First Double Bass? — We cannot name a person who made the first double bass as we know it today. Rather than being invented, the instrument evolved from others in use at the time to one that could produce a new range of lower notes than those available from existing instruments. Makers of double bass-like instruments appeared in many different parts of Europe. Early similar instruments were shaped like a violone with "C" rather than "*f*" shaped tone holes and had three strings. Their evolution is undocumented, but different sizes and numbers of strings were used.

16th Century — Larger violones in the viola da gamba family began to develop to provide for the lower notes. With this growth, the instrument's tuning number of strings and shapes was not standardized. At this time, the instrument had five or six strings.

17th Century — During this period, experimentation with three and four-string ass instruments resulted in various tunings.

18th – 19th Century — As the instrumentation of orchestras changed and increased in size, it was necessary to increase the double bass volume and range. To accommodate this need for more volume and range, some basses in Italy and England were made with three strings. These produced a more powerful sound however were limited in range. French and German luthiers took a different direction by making instruments with five strings.

20th Century — The four-string double bass as we know it now makes its appearance. The volume output of these instruments was less. However, an increase in the number of basses in an orchestra compensated for that loss. The result was an instrument that satisfied the needs of the music world.

Possible credit might be given for the beginnings of a bass string instrument to the renowned virtuoso of the viola da gamba Silvestro Ganassi. In about 1542, Silvestro expanded the viola da gamba to one that played in a lower register than those in existence.

Gasparo da Salo of Brescia, Italy (C.1540-1609) and Andrea Amati of Cremona, Italy (C.1525-1611) were luthiers making double basses at about the same time. We do not know who was first, so let's give them all credit for being among the first luthiers to make double basses. The objective was to create a powerful lower-pitched sound. However, the instruments were not well accepted because of the high cost of making them.

When considering the development of the double bass, it is quite evident that many things happened in many places throughout the centuries that finally settled on the instrument we now know. It was a long journey, but we did arrive with an instrument that serves many musical needs, from jazz to the symphony.

Lesson Four

The Schools

When you hear the word school, you will probably think of the building you go to for your double bass lesson or to study other subjects. The word school can also have another meaning. A school can be where people interested in a subject, such as double bass making, gather and live in a particular area to practice their art. The goal is to develop their skills and broaden their subject knowledge.

The string instrument makers from the mid-fifteen hundreds to about 1725 gathered in "schools," where they developed and refined the double bass to become the instrument we know and enjoy today.

Over some 200 years, such schools began to appear throughout Europe. The Brescian, Cremonese, Neapolitan, Tyrolean, and French schools were among them. Each is named for the geographic location where it was centered.

Timeline — Below is a timeline showing the location of some of these "schools" in Europe and those who worked there.

(C.1784-1875)
Lupot, Vuillaume

(C.1620-1743)
Klotz, Stainer

Paris

Mittenwald

Absam
•Tyrol

Brescia

Cremona

Naples

Gasparo da Salo
Maggini, Rogeri
(C.1585-1895)

Amati, Bergonzi,* Gagliano,*
Guarneri, Ruggieri, Stradivari
(C. 1541-1744)

*Bergonzi & Gagliano worked in Cremona and Naples

Let's now look into where the luthiers worked and what they did.

Cremonese School — Cremona, Italy

Andrea Amati (1525-1611) was the principal figure in the Cremonese school of instrument making. His early works consisted of rebecs and other string instruments that preceded the double bass. Historians began to see evidence showing the development of other string family instruments. Andrea's family consisted of Antonio, Girolamo, Nicolo, and Girolamo II, all carrying on the Amati tradition of making extraordinary string instruments up to 1740. Many of the instruments they made are still being played.

Antonio Stradivari (1644 to 1737) was, and still is, the most famous violin, viola, and cello maker in history. In his mid-career, Antonio experimented with instrument sizes to develop a cello that became the prototype for other luthiers building the instrument at that time. During his lifetime Stradivari made more than one thousand instruments.

Francesco Ruggieri (1620-1695) In addition to his work on violins and violas, Ruggieri is recognized for improving the design of the cello. His work became the basis on which today's cellos are made.

Carlo Bergonzi (1683-1747) was a neighbor and then a student of Stradivari. Bergonzi became Stradivari's repair technician.

Brescian School — Brescia, Italy

Brescia is the second-largest city in the Lombardy region of northern Italy, at the base of the Alps. Between 1585 and 1895, Brescia became a center for master luthiers. In Brescia, the Viola da Braccio (of the arm), viola da gamba (of the leg), and many other viols that had evolved up to that time became the models for the cello and double bass. The luthiers of the Brescian school were considered among the best instrument makers. Unfortunately, an outbreak of a deadly disease spread throughout the region, killing most of the population.

Gasparo da Salo (1542-1609) — Gasparo developed an assortment of string instruments, including violone, a general term used for larger string instruments. In this category, we would see the beginnings of early double bass-like instruments. He also made other string instruments in the violin, viola, and cello categories and developed a longer-shaped violin that produced a more forceful sound. Gasparo was a double bass player of some note.

Giovanni Paolo Maggini (1580-1630) —Maggini became a student of Gasparo da Salo. At about twenty years of age, Maggini developed his double bass designs with larger sound holes and a lower curving top. Maggini made about seventy-five instruments, mostly violins and violas, two cellos, and what might be one of the first double basses.

Neapolitan School — Naples, Italy

In the south of Italy, the area of Naples was growing. This growth increased the demand for musical instruments, resulting in the development of the Neapolitan School of instrument making.

Alessandro Gagliano (1640-1725) — Alessandro Gagliano and his family made instruments for almost three hundred years until 1925. Alessandro was the head of the family and is known for developing a brilliantly clear varnish with a beautiful red tint.

Tyrolean School — Mittenwald, Germany

During that same period, the Tyrolean School grew where Jacob Stainer (1620-1683) and Matthias Klotz (1656-1743) were the most important luthiers.

Jacob Stainer (1620-1683) was one of the most important luthiers of his time. He developed a design for his instruments that featured a higher arch on the top and back. He was also noted for his unique scrolls, which often featured carved heads instead of the traditional scroll shape.

Matthias Klotz (1656-1743) used his business skills to develop a complete string instrument industry. Like the Gagliano family, Klotz's business also became the family business, producing many instruments still available today.

French School — Mirecourt, France

In 1635 there were 43 luthiers in Mirecourt, France. About a century and a half later, Nicholas Lupot (1784-1824) and Jean-Baptiste Vuillaume (1798-1875) were best known for producing excellent string instruments based on the designs of previous masters. By the 20th Century, Mirecourt had become the center of the string instrument-making business.

Nicholas Lupot (1784-1824) was most noted for copying the Stradivari design and designs of other masters. Nicholas did not distinguish himself so much for his originality but rather for the delicate refinement he added to the patterns of others.

Jean-Baptiste Vuillaume (1798-1875) was able to copy the styles and varnishes of the master luthiers of the past. In 1828 he started his own business where he sold his reproductions and other high-quality instruments.

Summary — The "schools" of string instrument making mentioned above are only some of many that came into being throughout Europe beginning in the sixteenth Century. Venice and Absam (Austria) schools and other lesser-known clusters of luthiers on every level developed the violin, viola, cello, and double bass as we know them today.

We cannot say when and where the double bass first appeared. The rebab, rebec, vielle, viola da gamba, and viola da braccio, along with all the experimental instruments that came and went over the centuries, paved the way for luthiers to settle on the violin, viola, cello, and double bass as the four instruments that satisfied the musical needs of performers. These instruments now provide a complete range of notes with timbres (tone quality) that are harmonious and complementary to one another and permit performers to play with great ease and musicianship. The references above are only an introduction to some of the luthiers of the time. A search on the internet will tell you much more about their work and lives.

NOTES

Chapter 7

How Are Double Bass Bows Made?

Introduction — A double bass bow looks like a stick with hair attached. It is made up of between thirteen and fifteen parts. The parts we see most easily are the stick, hair, and frog. Not easily seen are the hidden parts that keep the bow together.

As you read this chapter, have your bow handy and look at each bow part as it is discussed.

The Materials — The materials needed to make a bow are:

1. wood for the stick, usually Pernambuco, with a straight, dense gain
2. ebony for the frog
3. metal for the fittings
4. a sheet of mother of pearl for the slides
5. a few hardwood plugs and wedges and
6. a hank of horsehair.

The Stick — The first step in making a bow is choosing the wood for the stick. The best bows are usually made with Pernambuco, a hardwood grown in Brazil. The bow maker (archetier) starts with a rectangular strip of wood the length of the bow. This is called a straight blank, which is then checked for defects in the grain, such as a knot or wormhole.

https://fiddlershop.com/blog/Pernambuco-Double bass-Bow-info

The blank is then roughly formed into an eight-sided (octagonal) or round shape.

The Head or Tip — After the stick is formed, the bow maker carves the tip of the bow.

When the tip is completed, a bone or plastic tip plate is glued in place, and a hole (mortise) is cut into its base to hold the tip end of the hair.

A mortise (hole) is cut into the other end of the stick to fit the frog.

The Frog — The bow maker begins shaping a blank piece of ebony wood into a shape that is wider on the bottom than at the top. The sides of the frog are shaped to curve slightly inward.

A mortise is cut into the frog, where the bow hair will be placed. Below is a frog with a mortise cut out and ready to accept hair.

The front of the frog will then be shaped into a "U," which faces the tip of the bow.

Below is a finished frog with the hair installed. The arrow points to a metal half-round band called a ferrule, placed over the end of the frog to hold the wooden wedge and hair in place.

 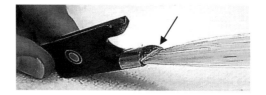

On the underside of the frog behind the ferrule is a mother-of-pearl slide (A), which covers the mortise and holds the bow hair in place. Continuing from that slide is a silver plate (B) that travels up the back of the frog to its top. A mother-of-pearl eye (C) is placed on either side of the frog as a decoration.

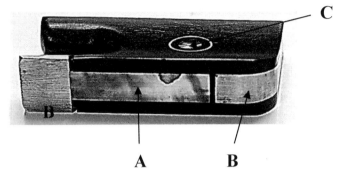

Fitting the Frog — The top of the frog is shaped to fit the stick. A metal strip called an underslide is placed on the top of the frog to strengthen it, ease its sliding back and forth on the stick, help support it and prevent cracking.

When finished, the frog is made up of a screw and an eyelet with a button on the end of the screw. The eyelet is screwed into the top of the frog. The screw goes into the eyelet, and the button is used to turn the screw.

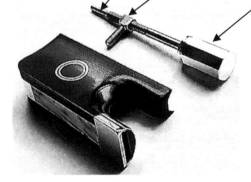

Creating the Curve (Camber) in a Bow Stick — The bow maker (archetier) heats the stick using a soft flame from an alcohol lamp to put the curve in a bow stick. When the stick has reached the proper temperature, it will begin to bend more easily. At that point, it is pressed against a form until it takes on the curve needed. The stick is then cooled and will keep the curved shape.

The Bow Grip — Just forward of the frog on the stick is a wrapping or bow grip that can be made of almost any material wrapped around a stick. Below are pictured leather, whalebone, and silver wraps.

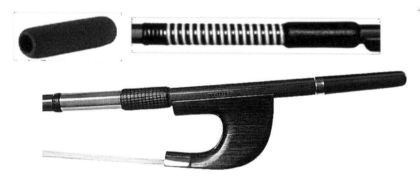

Completing the Stick — Let's review the work that has been done up to this point:

1. The archetier started with a "blank" strip of wood for the stick.
2. The stick was carved and shaped.
3. A frog was cut from a block of ebony wood.
4. A mortise was cut into the block to receive the bow hair.
5. The metal parts were added to the frog.
6. The tip of the stick was carved and shaped.
7. A bone or ivory tip was glued onto the tip.
8. A mortise was cut into the tip to receive the bow hair.
9. The stick was heated and curved to create a proper camber.
10. A grip was added to the stick just forward of the frog.

Hairing the Bow — The next step is hairing the bow. Use the diagram below and your own bow as a guide while you read about the process.

To hair, a bow, a hank of horsehair (A) is combed, so all hairs are parallel. One end of the hank is then tied and forced securely into a box-shaped cutout (mortise) at the tip of the bow (B). The hair is held in place by a wooden, wedge-shaped plug (C) that is cut to exactly fit the space and hold the hair in place.

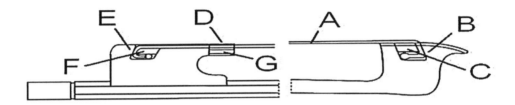

A ferrule (metal band) (D) is placed over the hair, which is stretched along the bow, tied at the other end, and set into a box-shaped cutout in the frog (E). A wooden wedge-shaped plug is placed into the box (F) to keep the hair in place. A slide and another wooden wedge are placed between the ferrule and the frog (G) to help distribute the hairs equally and keep them in place.

The archetier will make the stick's final adjustments to ensure it is straight, balanced, flexible, has the proper camber, and that the frog works properly. The stick will then be colored and polished.

Summary — A bow is an important part of producing sound on a double bass. For this reason, the quality of the hair and wood used, how the wood is formed into a well-balanced stick with proper camber (curve), and correct weight and balance are most important.

Chapter 8

What Is the History of Bows?

The idea of making sound by rubbing something with a rough surface against a tight string might be how the very earliest bow came to be. Drawings dating as far back as the eighth-century show chords and hair tied or connected in different ways to bow-shaped sticks.

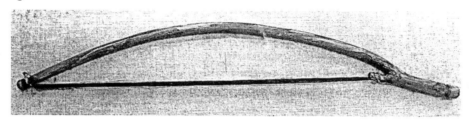

This arrangement would allow the chords or hairs to be rubbed against a tight string, causing it to vibrate and produce a sound. Drawings of bows can be found in many different shapes. The one thing they all have in common is a curved stick that would hold a chord-like material or hair.

There is very little information on the early history of bows. Sculptures and paintings from the past hint at the double bass size, shape, structure, and playing positions, but those same works of art give little information about the bows. We might guess that the artists either did not know the important role bows had in sound production or that the bow was, in their minds, not important enough to deserve more detailed attention.

Beginning in the early 1600s, cello music changed from background rhythms to the melody. Playing rhythmic patterns required a simple bow that was short and had a wider arc, whereas to play the melody, musicians needed a more flexible, graceful overhand bow grip.

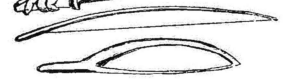

This hand position and a longer, better-balanced bow gave the player greater control. By using these newer designed bows, musicians produced various sounds ranging from very smooth and sensitive to crisp short separated notes. The bow sticks became straighter, lighter, and better balanced, and the frog that controlled the tension of the hair was more refined.

The master archetier (bow maker), Eitan Hoffer, operates a shop in Israel where he makes bows for ancient instruments. Below are some pictures of Mr. Hoffer's bows which illustrate the shapes that came before the bows we now use.

The following examples of ancient bows were reproduced with the permission of Eitan Hoffer, Bow Maker.

Renaissance Viol Bow Made from yew wood.

 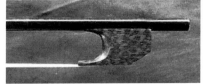

Short Viol Bow
Copy of an original Italian bow produced at the end of the 16th Century.

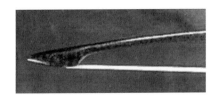 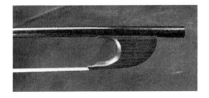

17th Century Style Bow
Made from snakewood, this bow is almost 26 inches long.

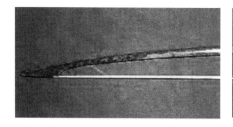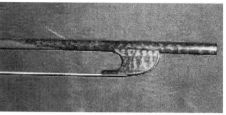

17th Century Short Bow

A reproduction of a bow from the year 1680. Look at
the difference in the size of the frog compared to the bow above.

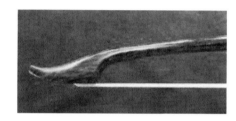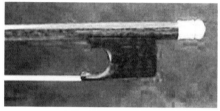

French 18th Century Bow with Screw Mechanism

This is an early snakewood bow with a movable frog.

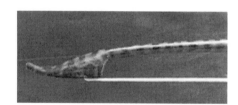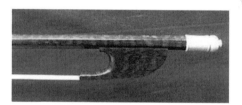

Viola "Long Sonata Bow" (c. 1720)

A copy of the original bow used for playing early 18th-century music like that of J. S. Bach.

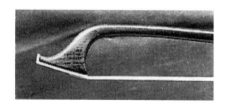

Classical Bow

Based on an original bow by N. Duchaine (c. 1765).

The Bows You Now Use

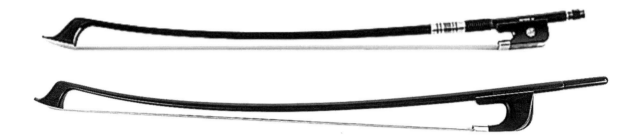

The bow you use is an important part of the sound-making process. You use your bow to control the tone quality, clarity, volume, phrasing, and all the musical sounds you are making. You, your bow, and your double bass are partners in the act of making music. Because of the importance of this three-way partnership, you must credit those bowmakers from the past who improved the ancient bows you saw above to develop the bow you now use.

François Xavier Tourte (1747-1835) had a great effect on developing the bow you use today. Trained to make string instruments by his father, Nicolas Pierre (1700-1765), François also began work on improving the bow. He changed the balance, increased the frog's weight and tip, and changed the bow's length. Tourte also refined the process for creating the camber (curve) in the bow stick by using heat instead of the carving method used at that time.

Added to that list of improvements, François invented the moveable frog using the screw and eye mechanism, which you now use to tighten or loosen your bow hair. He also developed a method to spread the hairs at the frog with a wedge of wood inserted between the hair and the ferrule. This small but very important addition resulted in the individual hairs being firmly held parallel to one another rather than clumping. (For a detailed view of these bow parts, see lesson 5 in Chapter 1).

An interesting story about François tells about his passion for perfection. François would destroy any bow made in his shop, which was not perfect in his judgment. The result was the possible loss of some great bows which, although not perfect enough in his eyes to enjoy life, would probably serve us as great tools. His bow design became the model for all the prominent bow makers to follow.

The three most famous bowmakers after Tourte were Ludwig Bausch (1805-1871), François Voirin (1833-1885), and Eugene Sartory (1871-1946).

Ludwig Christian August Bausch (1805-1871) followed Tourte as a maker of excellent bows. Ludwig lived and worked in Germany, where he and his two sons carried on the Tourte fine bow-making art until 1874.

François Nicolas Voirin (1833-1885) was a French maker of bows that many string instrument players feel were the best made. Voirin redesigned the Tourte bow by thinning out the tip, changing the camber (curve) of the stick, and making it thinner at the heel (frog end).

Eugene Nicolas Sartory (1871-1946) was also a French maker of fine bows. His bows were made with stronger, thicker sticks and wider tips than the bows made by Voirin and Bausch.

Unlike the bows for the violin, viola, and cello, which had a relatively smooth transition into being standardized, double bass bow sizes and designs evolved differently. Early lower-string instruments' sizes and playing techniques were far from consistent, resulting in an extraordinary variety of bows.

The hair tension on earlier bows before frogs were invented was controlled by the player's overhand grip, which enabled thumb pressure to be exerted on the hair. Pressing on the hair gives a tighter ribbon, whereas releasing the thumb loosens the hair. Francois Xavier Tourte (1747-1835) solved that problem by inventing the adjustable frog we now use.

With the onset of the romantic period in music, changes in orchestra sizes and instrumentation created a demand for various bow sizes and designs. Double bass makers had established some consistency in design lengths, weights, camber, stock wood, and personal preference, creating a period of experimentation that resulted in the French and German bows that are commonly used today.

Summary — At some point in the development of civilization, it was learned that rubbing a rough stick against a tight string would produce a sound. Ancient drawings and paintings which contain pictures of instruments and their bows show bow-shaped sticks with hair or chords connected to the stick on both ends. A musician could rub that chord or hair against a tight string and produce sound. From then on, people's creative ability took over to develop the bows you use to play your double bass today. You will enjoy more information on their lives and achievements if you research each of the luthiers mentioned above.

Chapter 9

A Dictionary for Double Bass Students

During your studies, you will come across unfamiliar words related to your double bass or bow. This dictionary lists some of the words in alphabetical order and their meanings.

Terms Used for Bowing Directions

The universal language for music is Italian; however, other languages are also used.

Arco (Italian) — Use the bow to play this section.

Au Talon (French) — Play this passage at the frog end of the bow.

Avec le Bois (French) — Use the bow stick in place of the bow hair to bow the string.

Bow — An arch-shaped stick with horsehair or manufactured hair stretched from one end of the stick to the other. The hair is drawn across a string to produce sound.

Brazilwood — A type of wood used to make bows.

Col Legno Battuto (Italian) — Strike the string with the wooden bow stick using a bouncing motion.

Collé (French) — Use a light short bow stroke. Attack from above using a brief contact with the string followed by a clean release upward.

Col Legno Tratto (Italian) — Use the bow stick in place of the bow hair to bow the string.

Détaché (French) — Bow detached notes smoothly without pausing between them.

Détaché Lance (French) — Bow detached notes smoothly with a slight pause between them.

Flautando (Italian) — Bow close to or slightly over the fingerboard edge. This will modify the sound to resemble that of a flute. (See Sul Tasto below.)

Jeté (French) — "Throw" (bounce) the bow across the string to produce a series of short notes. Like skipping a rock across water.

Legato (Italian) — Use a smooth bowing motion with no break between notes, except for pitch changes.

Marcato (Italian) — Use a strong, bold bow stroke.

Martelé (French) — Use a strong accented attack to the note with immediate release.

Martellato (Italian) — Italian for martelé. Use a strong accented attack to the note with immediate release.

Pernambuco — A wood grown in South America. This wood is considered to be the finest for making bows.

Pizzicato (Italian) — Pluck the string.

Ponticello (Italian) — Direct the bowing close to the bridge to produce a stronger sound. See Sul Ponticello below.

Punta d'arco (Italian) — Direct the bowing to the tip of the bow to produce a softer sound.

Ricochet (French) — Bounce the bow off the string in a series of notes.

Rosin — Tree resin in a solid form applied to bow hair to make it sticky.

Sautillé (French) — Use a light bow stroke bouncing across the string.

Spiccato (Italian) — Use a bouncing bow stroke across the string to produce very short separated notes.

Staccato (Italian) — Produce a short note using any of the "separated note" techniques listed.

Sul (Italian) — Sul means "on." It also indicates "near" as in "sul ponticello."

Sul Ponticello (Italian) — Bow near the bridge to produce a stronger sound.

Tasto (Italian) — The fingerboard.

Sul Tasto (Italian) — Bow over or near the fingerboard to produce a softer sound.

Tremolo (Italian) — Repeat the same note by rapidly moving the bow back and forth with a wrist motion.

Trill — Fast back-and-forth changing of two notes a half or whole step apart.

Vibrato (Italian) — A repeated fast slight change in pitch.

NOTES

Chapter 10

A Review of Double Bass Parts and Their Use

Back — The back of the body of the double bass, also called the backplate.

Bass Bar — A strip of wood on the underside of the top of the double bass, reinforcing the top and distributing the lower notes throughout the top.

Belly — The top of a double bass, sometimes called the top plate.

Bridge — A support for the strings on a double bass. The bridge transfers sound from a vibrating string to the instrument's top.

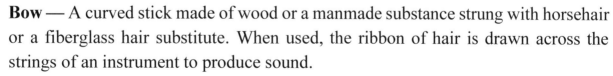

Bow — A curved stick made of wood or a manmade substance strung with horsehair or a fiberglass hair substitute. When used, the ribbon of hair is drawn across the strings of an instrument to produce sound.

Bow Hair — Horsehair or a manmade substitute strung across a bow.

Body — The main part of a double bass. The body (front, sides, and back) strengthens the sound produced by the vibrating strings.

Block — A wooden block placed at key points in the body of a string instrument to 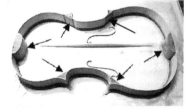 strengthen the unit. One block is placed in each corner where the upper and lower bouts meet the C bout. One block is placed at the bottom of the body to reinforce the endpin, and one block is placed at the top to reinforce the neck contact.

Bout— The word used to identify the three sections of a string instrument's body. The upper third is called the upper bout, the middle section is called the C bout, and the lower third is called the lower bout.

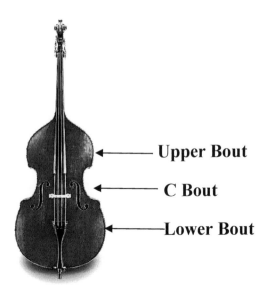

Upper Bout

C Bout

Lower Bout

100

Endpin — An adjustable metal rod inserted at the end of a double bass that rests on the floor to support the instrument.

"ƒ" Hole —Sometimes called a sound hole, an **"ƒ"** hole is an **"ƒ"** shaped opening in the top of a double bass that allows sound vibrations to escape from the instrument.

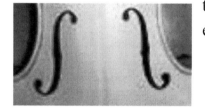

Fine Tuner — A device built into a tailpiece that, when turned, will slightly adjust the pitch of a string.

Fingerboard — A hardwood board (usually ebony) that extends from the pegbox to provide a surface against which you can press the string to change pitches.

Ferrule — A metal band called a ferrule placed over the hair at the end of a bow frog.

Lining — Thin strips of wood glued around the inside edge of the ribs of a string instrument to strengthen it.

Mute — A device placed on the bridge to change a sound's tone quality and volume.

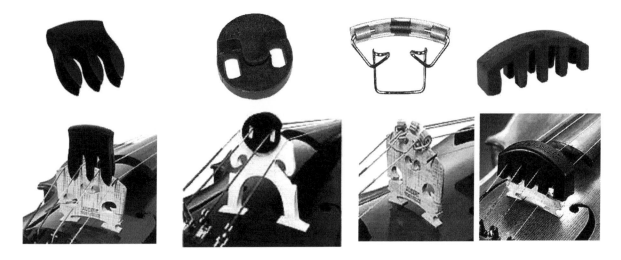

Nut — The wooden insert over which the strings pass from the pegbox to the fingerboard.

Peg — Another term for a machine head, the mechanism used to adjust string tension on a double bass.

Purfling — Two parallel strips of hardwood, usually ebony, inlaid into the edge of the top and back of a string instrument to strengthen the edges and control vibration.

Ribs — The sides of a double bass.

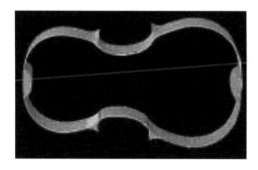

Saddle — A hardwood bar placed at the end of the top of a double bass to support the tailgut and prevent damage to the body.

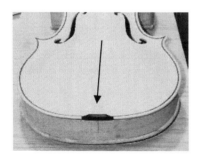

Soundpost — A wooden dowel (post) that supports the top of the double bass and conducts the vibrations the higher strings produce from the top of the double bass to its back.

Scroll — The decorative top of a double bass.

Scroll Eye — The center of a scroll.

Tailpiece — A device to which double bass string's lower ends are attached. Some tailpieces have fine tuners built into them.

Tailgut — A short piece of gut or nylon that secures the tailpiece to the endpin.

Wolf Tone Eliminator — Eliminates the wobbling tone that sometimes happens, often on the G# on some double basses.

Index

accessories, 39-52

adjustments, 26-27, 33

Amati, 53-54, 76, 78-79

bass bar, 5, 7, 9, 60, 99

bib, 52

bow, 12-15

bowed instruments, 71-73

Brescian School, 77-80

bridge, 3, 5-7, 9, 26-29, 33, 64,99

care, 25-27

    bow, 31-32

    cases, 32

    double bass, 25-27

Cremonese School, 77-79

double bass (made), 53-68

electronic tuners, 11, 40-41

endpin, 4, 9, 65, 73, 100-101,

    anchor, 42

    stop, 42

    wheel, 48

"f"-holes, 5-7, 9, 27, 59-60, 72, 75,

    101

ferrule, 14, 85-86, 88, 92, 101

fine tuners, 30, 41, 101, 104

fingering chart, 16-23

finish, 25, 52, 66-68

French School, 77, 81

history,

    bows, 89-94

    double bass, 69-81

hook, 48

horsehair, 13, 83, 88, 95, 99-100

humidifiers, 49

kantele, 69

lira da braccio, 75

lute, 70

lyre, 70-71

machine head, 2, 10, 29, 54, 65, 103

music stands, 50

mutes, 44, 102

Neapolitan School, 77, 80

nut, 2,15, 28-30, 33, 64 69-70, 102

open strings, 10

pegbox, 2, 29-30, 61-63, 70, 72-73, 75,

    101-102

pitch pipes, 11, 40

pitch notation, viii

plucked instruments, 69-71

purfling, 5, 8-9, 53, 58, 103

quiver, 47

rebab, 72-74

rebec, 73-74, 79, 81

rock stop, 42

rosin, 39, 96

saddle, 4, 64, 103

scroll, 61-62, 80, 104

set up, 54, 64, 66

sides (double bass), 5, 7, 9, 53-54, 57,

    100, 103

  soundpost, 5-7, 9, 28, 59, 65, 104

spike fiddle, 73

Stradivari, 78-79. 81

strings, 5, 7, 10, 15, 33, 42-43

tailpiece, 4, 26, 28-30, 33, 41, 43, 53,

    63, 65, 70, 101, 104

Tyrolean School, 77, 80-81

transport device, 48

tuning, 2, 10-12, 15, 36-37, 41, 43,
  59-60

tuning fork 40

vibration, 9, 40, 58-59, 101, 103-104

vielle, 73-75, 81

wolf tone, 44, 105

zither, 70-72